Guess Who?

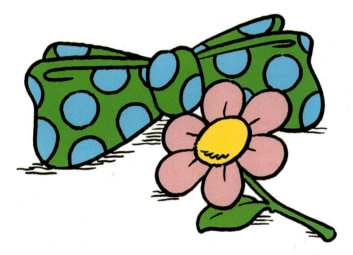

Paul Shipton
Illustrated by Andy Hammond

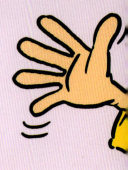

I put on my shirt.

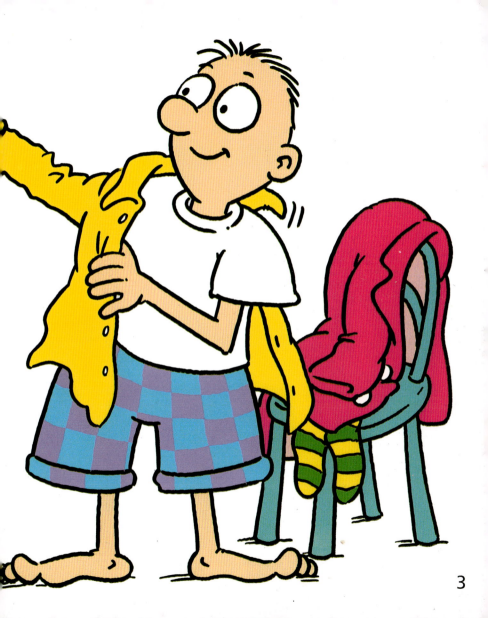

I put on my tie.

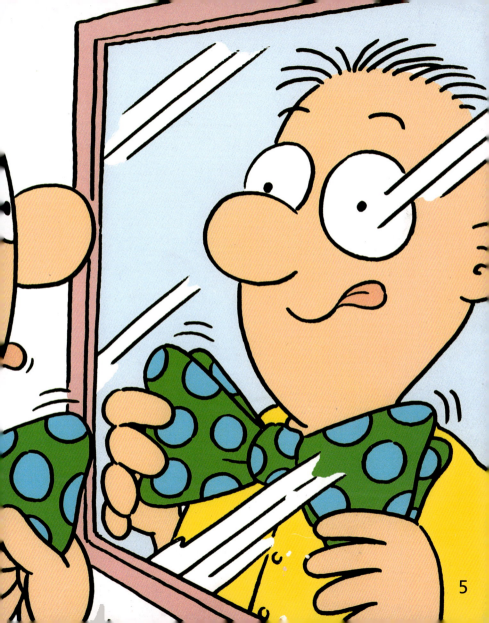

I put on my coat.

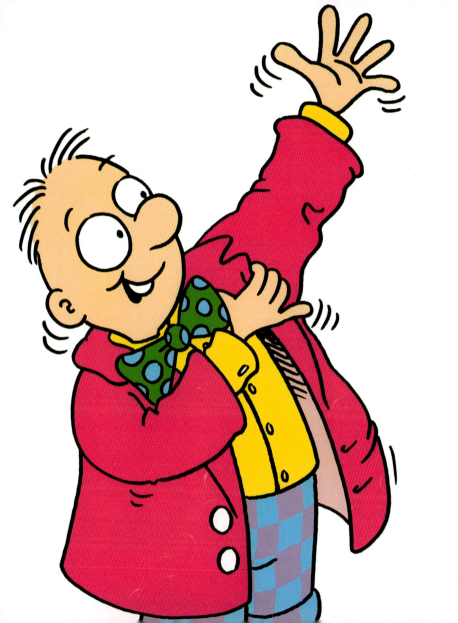

I put on my socks.

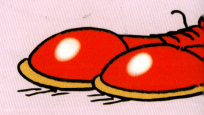

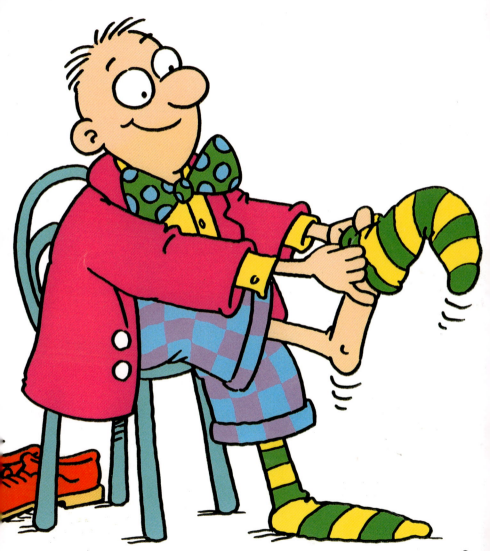

I put on my shoes.

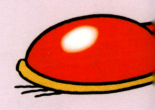

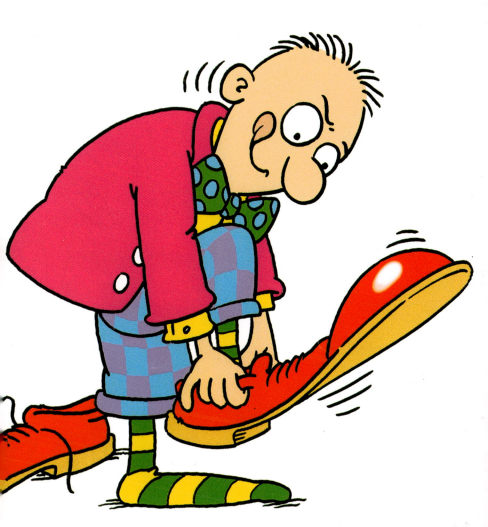

I put on my wig.

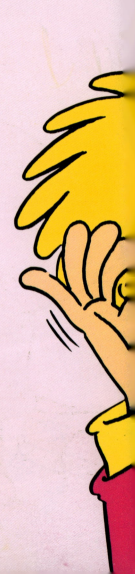

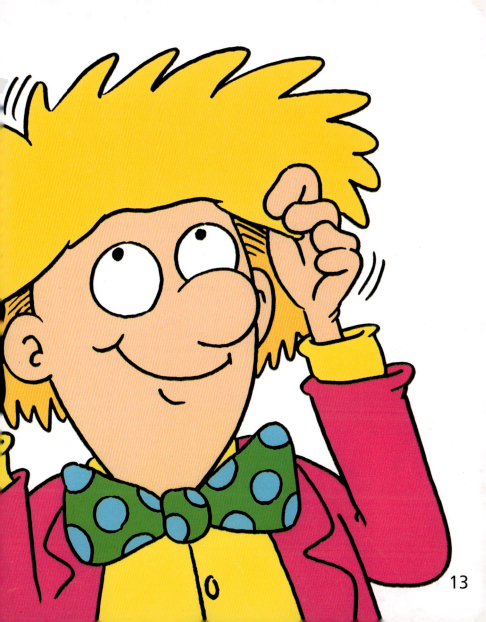

I put on my hat.

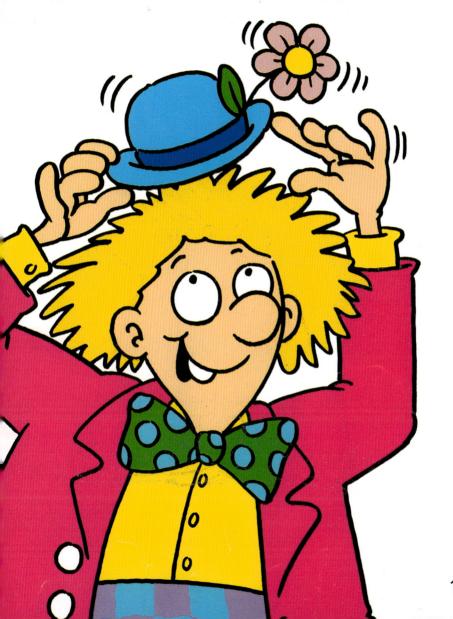

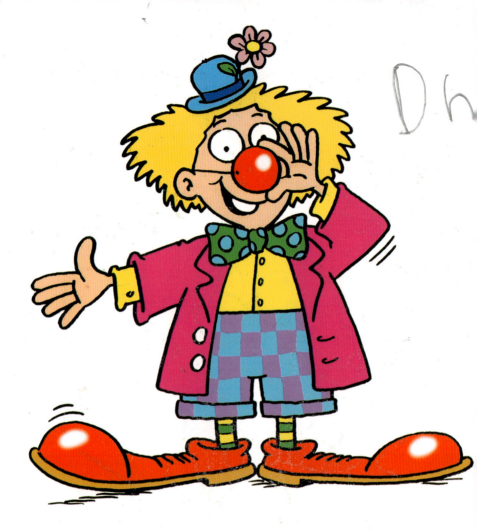

I put on my nose!